WORLD SOCCER LEGENDS

BEFORE THEY WERE STARS

Abbeville Press Publishers
New York · London

A portion of this book's proceeds are donated to the Hugo Bustamante AYSO Playership Fund, a national scholarship program to help ensure that no child misses the chance to play AYSO Soccer. Donations to the fund cover the cost of registration and a uniform for a child in need.

Text by Illugi Jökulsson
Design and layout: Árni Torfason

For the English-language edition
Copy editor: Ken Samelson
Production editor: Matt Garczynski
Composition: Ada Rodriguez
Production manager: Louise Kurtz

PHOTOGRAPHY CREDITS

Getty Images: front cover left (Luis Bagu), pp. 6–7 and back cover top (Popperfoto), 8 (Philippe Le Tellier), 10–11 (Bob Thomas), 12 (Mark Leech/Offside), 14–15 (Bob Donnan), 16–17 (Will McIntyre), 18–19 (Christian Liewig – Corbis), 20 (Mark Francotte), 22–23 (Mark Leech/Offside), 24 (Shaun Botterill/Allsport), 26–27 (Al Tielemans/Sports Illustrated), 28 (Brian Bahr), 30–31 and back cover bottom (VI-Images), 32 (VI-Images), 34–35 (Simon Bruty), 36 (Stephen Dunn), 38–39 (Ben Radford), 40 (Alice Leafblad/SSP/Ssp/The LIFE Images Collection), 42–43 (Al Messerschmidt), 44–45 and back cover center (Ben Radford), 46–47 (Bagu Blanco), 48 (Nadine Rupp), 50–51 (Collegiate Images), 54–55 (Jeff Zelevansky), 56 (Lintao Zhang), 58–59 (Aurelien Meunier), 62–63 (Jamie McDonald – FIFA)

Shutterstock: p. 52 and front cover right (Santiago Llanquin/AP), 60 (A. Ricardo)

First published in the United States of America in 2019 by Abbeville Press, 655 Third Avenue, New York, NY 10017

First Edition
10 9 8 7 6 5 4 3 2 1

ISBN 978-0-7892-1327-3

Library of Congress Cataloging-in-Publication Data available upon request

For bulk and premium sales and for text adoption procedures, write to Customer Service Manager, Abbeville Press, 655 Third Avenue, New York, NY 10017, or call 1-800-ARTBOOK.

Visit Abbeville Press online at www.abbeville.com.

CONTENTS

PELÉ

What's in a name?

Brazilians are famous for referring to their soccer legends by their first name or even a nickname. One nickname, though, rules them all and is known to every soccer fan on the planet. That is the name of the legendary Pelé, who played the leading role in bringing three World Cup titles to the Brazilian national team out of four attempts between 1958 and 1970. He is unquestionably one of the greatest footballers ever.

But where does the famous nickname come from? Pelé's given name is Edson, in honor of the American inventor Thomas Alva Edison. Young Edson was called "Dico" by his family, and his close relatives and friends used that name all his life. When Pelé began playing soccer, he was for a time known as "Gasolina," in reference to a famous Brazilian singer. Writing about the latter name in his biography, Pelé said, "Thankfully, that didn't last."

The name "Pelé" is probably derived from the fact that his father, a

Pelé's father, Dondinho, played soccer professionally, but in those days it was not a means to riches. The family was poor, and Dondinho could not even afford to buy his son a proper soccer ball. Pelé was enthralled by the sport from a very early age, and it was all he wanted to do. He played in the streets with his friends, who came from families similar to his. They would stuff a sock with newspapers and tie the open end, and this would serve as a makeshift ball. They sometimes even played soccer using a grapefruit. Through these experimental ways of playing soccer, the young Pelé taught himself countless ways to express his skills.

Pele, age 17, during a brief stint as goalkeeper, 1957.

Pelé, age 17, on the day of his first World Cup Final appearance, June 29, 1958.

moderately successful soccer player, often spoke about his friend, a goalkeeper named Bilé. When Edson was a young child, he once accompanied his father to the soccer field and told his father's teammates that one day he "would become a goalkeeper just like Bilé." They misheard him and thought he had said Pelé, and from then on the name stuck to the boy. He originally hated the nickname, and he was often teased because of it. Eventually he realized that his only option was to embrace the name and take pride in it. And then the name became one of the world's most familiar.

It is worth mentioning that despite Pelé's incredible skill as a goal scorer, he also loved playing the position of goalkeeper during practices. Turns out he was also quite skilled in that role—just like Bilé!

In his early teens, Pelé joined a youth squad coached by Waldemar de Brito, himself a former forward for the Brazilian national team. After leading the squad to two state youth championships, Pelé was encouraged to try out for the professional club Santos FC. Coach de Brito assured Santos that his newly discov-

EDSON ARANTES DO NASCIMENTO, KNOWN AS PELÉ
DATE OF BIRTH: OCTOBER 23, 1940
PLACE OF BIRTH: TRÊS CORAÇÕES, MINAS GERAIS, BRAZIL
YOUTH CLUB: BAURU (1953–56)
SENIOR CLUBS: SANTOS (1956–74), NEW YORK COSMOS (1975–77)
NATIONAL TEAM: BRAZIL (1957–71)

ered phenom was destined to become "the greatest football player in the world," a prophecy that would soon be fulfilled.

Pelé scored his first professional goal for Santos before his sixteenth birthday, and was granted a starting spot on the first team in the 1957 season. He quickly became the top scorer in the league. Just ten months into his professional career, Pelé was called up to compete on the Brazilian national team. To this day he remains the youngest player to play in a World Cup final match, at just 17 years and 249 days old. He scored two goals in a 5–2 victory against Sweden, dazzling soccer fans all around the world. Edson's four-letter moniker was about to become a household name.

Pelé was one of the few soccer players of his time to develop his abilities by playing indoor soccer. After his talents had become evident and he was pulled from the streets by an organized soccer team, for a while he played only indoor soccer, which is known in Brazil as futebol de salão, or futsal. Reminiscing about his indoor soccer days, Pelé would later say, "It was through futebol de salão that I first got my chance to play with adults. . . . That gave me a lot of confidence. I knew then not to be afraid of whatever might come." That fearlessness would stick with Pelé throughout his life—he was never afraid of anything or anyone!

MARADONA

Many soccer stars were born in abject poverty and then worked hard to earn a living and improve their lives, using their particular kind of genius. That is certainly the case with Diego Armando Maradona, the Argentine forward recognized as the world's greatest soccer player from 1985 to 1990. He was so agile and skillful that he managed to shape a subpar Argentine team into the 1986 world champions. In the mind of most soccer fans, Maradona competes with his countryman Leo Messi and the Brazilian Pelé for the title of the greatest soccer player of all time.

When Maradona was born in 1960, his family's situation did not forecast a promising future for the boy. They were extremely poor and lived in

Maradona started playing soccer as a little boy on the streets of Villa Fiorito. He was short and skinny and therefore had to rely on his agility and low center of gravity to dribble past the bigger boys. Eventually, he came to outperform even the older kids, and earned a reputation as coach Francis Cornejo's secret weapon during games. Cornejo once entered the twelve-year-old in a game under the fictitious name "Montanya" to hide the fact that he was too young to play. When the rival coach caught on to the scheme, he cried, "You played Maradona . . . I'll let it go this time, I'm not going to report you. You really are lucky. That kid is wonderful."

Maradona, age 18, crosses the ball into Holland's penalty area during the FIFA 75th Anniversary Match in Berne, Switzerland, May 22, 1979.

Maradona celebrates an assist in Scotland, June 2, 1979. It was during this game that the 18-year-old scored his first goal for Argentina.

the slum of Villa Fiorito in Buenos Aires, the capital of Argentina. His parents had both moved to the city from a modest rural town in order to make a better life for themselves, but they faced many hardships. They lived in a small apartment along with other relatives. They had eight children, of whom Maradona was the fourth, and the oldest son. Maradona and his siblings all slept together in a tiny room in the apartment.

One night, Maradona got lost in the dark and fell into the family cesspit. Fortunately, his uncle Cirilo, who lived with the family, was able to rescue him, screaming at him, "Diegito, keep your head above [it]!" Maradona would later recount the story when he was asked about his family's living conditions. He told the story with a grin, and then added, "It wasn't easy, eh? Nothing was easy."

A neighbor of the family in Villa Fiorito remembered that Maradona "had nothing else but football. He was not educated, he had no sophistication. He was shirtless and barefoot. He was just this street kid with a gift from God."

While playing for his local club Estrella Roja, he caught the eye of a youth scout and was recruited to Las Cebollitas (The Little Onions), the junior team of the Argentinos

Juniors. Coach Francisco Cornejo recalls, "When Diego came to Argentinos Juniors for trials, I was really struck by his talent and couldn't believe he was only eight years old. . . . Although he had the physique of a child, he played like an adult. When we discovered he'd been telling us the truth, we decided to devote ourselves purely to him."

With the Little Onions, Maradona won 140 straight games and led the team to a 1972 junior championship. He started working as a ball boy during first-division games, and would delight the crowds with demonstrations of his ball-handling skills at halftime. His professional debut for Argentinos Juniors came in 1976, and by the end of the season, he had become a staple of the team. During his five years on the Juniors, he scored 116 goals in 167 appearances.

Maradona began playing on an international level at sixteen. Unfortunately he was denied an exciting opportunity when the Argentine national team coach decided he was too young to compete in the 1978 World Cup. Maradona would put in an impressive performance in the 1979 FIFA U-20 World Cup, earning the Golden Ball and a championship win for Argentina. He and Messi are the only two players so far to win a Golden Ball for both the U-20 and regular World Cup.

The United States is now a powerhouse in women's soccer, but that was definitely not the case when Mia Hamm first started playing the sport. The role Hamm played in the rise of the U.S. women's team is all the more remarkable because she was born with a physical defect on one foot, known as a clubfoot. When she was only a few months old, she was given a special cast to help shape her foot, and then she had to wear corrective shoes.

Hamm was born in Selma, Alabama, and was the fourth of six children. Her father was a pilot in the U.S. Air Force, and the family would travel from one military base to the other. When Hamm was eighteen months old, her family moved to a base in Florence, Italy. Soccer is the Italian national sport, and one day Hamm went to see her father and brother play in a game. She eagerly demanded to join in, and despite her corrective shoes, it turned out that she had considerable skill and often managed to steal the soccer ball from her father and brother. And so she discovered her sport of choice and never looked back.

MIA HAMM

Hamm inherited her soccer abilities partly from her mother, Stephanie, who was a ballerina. In fact, Hamm's nickname "Mia" comes from her mother's ballet mentor, Mia Slavenska. Hamm's full name is Mariel Margaret Hamm.

Hamm, age 20, in the NCAA Women's
National Championship Finals
against Duke, November 22, 1992.

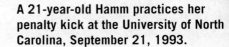

A 21-year-old Hamm practices her penalty kick at the University of North Carolina, September 21, 1993.

MARIEL MARGARET "MIA" HAMM
DATE OF BIRTH: MARCH 17, 1972
PLACE OF BIRTH: SELMA, ALABAMA
YOUTH CLUBS: NOTRE DAME KNIGHTS (1986–88), LAKE BRADDOCK BRUINS (1989)
COLLEGE CLUB: NORTH CAROLINA TAR HEELS (1989–93)
SENIOR CLUB: WASHINGTON FREEDOM (2001–03)
NATIONAL TEAM: UNITED STATES (1987–2004)

When Hamm was five, the family moved to Wichita Falls, Texas, where she joined her first soccer team. Her father served as coach, and one of her teammates was her newly adopted Thai-American brother, eight-year-old Garrett. Hamm's brother became both a playmate and a role model for her on the field.

Interviewed by CNN, Hamm's former youth coach John Cossaboon describes his impression of her as a young player: "Skinny, gangly, faster than the wind . . . The athleticism just jumped out at you and then, quickly after that, you could just see the natural instinct." Hamm was only fifteen when she became the youngest player ever to join the women's national team.

The Lake Braddock Secondary School in Virginia was lucky to have Hamm for a year, as she helped their team win a state championship. During her college career at the University of North Carolina at Chapel Hill from 1989 to 1993, the UNC Tar Heels were unstoppable. They won all four NCAA Division I women's soccer championships, and ninety-four of the ninety-five games that Hamm played in.

In the 1991 Women's World Cup, Hamm was the youngest player on the U.S. squad at just nineteen years old. She scored the decisive goal in the sixty-second minute of the first match, and a winning streak ensued. The U.S. brought home its first World Cup title that year, in part thanks to Mia's efforts.

Despite her many achievements, Hamm has also experienced her share of misfortune. Her beloved brother Garrett died from a rare blood disease in 1997. Hamm named her son after him and established the Mia Hamm Foundation, which encourages bone marrow donations and aids patients in need of bone marrow transplants.

France has boasted several great soccer teams, such as the one that entered the 1958 World Cup, where Just Fontaine scored thirteen goals and led his countryment to third place. And in 1984, Michel Platini and his companions became European champions. But it was not until 1984 that France won its first World Cup, thanks to a performance by Zinedine Zidane that caught the world's attention.

Zidane grew up in an impoverished suburb of Marseille, Cité de la Castellane, which is mainly populated by immigrants from North Africa, Sub-Saharan Africa, and the Caribbean. His parents hailed from the Kabylie region of northern Algeria and belonged to the Berber ethnic group. "My father taught me everything, but most of all he taught me the value of respect," Zidane remembered. "I had a strict upbringing, but he was a big guiding light, and I tried to apply this in my career."

In his youth, Zidane was called "Yazid," which is his middle name—the nickname by which we know him now, "Zizou," came along much later. Zidane had three brothers and one sister. He and his brothers would

ZINEDINE

ZIDANE

Zidane, age 22, during his first cap match playing for the French national team, 17 August, 1994. Coming in as a substitute in the 63rd minute, he went on to score two goals against the Czech team and tie the game 2–2.

ZINEDINE "ZIZOU" ZIDANE
DATE OF BIRTH: JUNE 23, 1972
PLACE OF BIRTH: MARSEILLE, FRANCE
YOUTH CLUBS: US SAINT HENRI (1981–83), SO SEPTÉMES-LES-VALLONS (1983–86), CANNES (1986–89)
SENIOR CLUBS: CANNES (1989–92), BORDEAUX (1992–96), JUVENTUS (1996–2001), REAL MADRID (2001–06)
NATIONAL TEAM: FRANCE (1994–2006)

Zidane, age 18, in uniform for AS Cannes, his first professional team, July 1, 1990.

play soccer with other neighborhood kids at the Place Tartane, a plaza close to his giant apartment building and the Casino super-market where his father worked. Zidane also practiced judo until the age of eleven, when soccer became his consuming passion.

Zidane began practicing with the neigh-borhood team AS Foresta but soon trans-ferred to a another team nearby, US Saint-Henri, where he was given the number 10 jersey, at the age of ten. He was very skilled with the soccer ball but was some-what lacking in strength and speed. Jean Varraud, a scout for the Cannes team, heard of Zidane's abilities and went on a special trip just to observe him play with his new team. Zidane played the position of libero (sweeper) in the defense, but managed to muck up a play that cost his team a goal. Yet Varraud saw something in him and decided to offer Zidane, who was then barely fifteen years old, a contract with Cannes. Cannes is more than eighty miles east of Marseille, so Zidane lived with a host family there. With Cannes, Zidane's talents began to shine, and he went on to become both a magician and a leader on the field.

The Uruguayan star Enzo Francescoli played the 1989–90 season with Marseille, and Zidane would journey to Stade Vélodrome as often as he could to watch him play. "I tried to imitate everything he did on the field," Zidane admitted. "He was extremely elegant."

When Zidane had a son, he named him Enzo. A year later he faced Francescoli on the field, and his idol offered him his jersey at the end of the game, saying, "This is for your son." Zidane himself wore this jersey to sleep for years, even during the 1998 World Cup tournament in France. Francescoli's jersey was eventually banned from the bedroom by Véronique, Zidane's wife. "I constantly have the feeling that I'm sleeping with a soccer player," she said.

Enzo Francescoli later introduced his own son to Zidane. Enzo's son asked Zidane what he had done to become so skilled. "Ask your dad" was the Frenchman's response. "I learned everything from him."

DAVID BEC

Even though David Beckham will always be associated with the city of Manchester, he was actually born in London. But the popularity of Manchester United reached far beyond its home city, and both of Beckham's parents, Sandra and Ted, were avid United fans in the seventies, despite residing in the capital. The team was not exactly triumphant in those days, but the Beckhams didn't mind. David was born in 1975, and soon after the family traveled to Manchester to watch their favorite team play. And so the boy learned at an early age that playing for Man U was the highest goal to which a footballer could aspire.

David Beckham's wife Victoria, also known as Posh Spice from the musical group the Spice Girls, claims that the

David Beckham is no less astute in the boardroom than he was on the field, as witnessed by the business empire he built following his retirement from soccer. When he was in school, however, Beckham was not interested in applying his intelligence to his studies. During a press interview, he said, "At school whenever teachers asked, 'What do you want to do when you're older?' I'd say, 'I want to be a footballer.' And they'd say, 'No, what do you really want to do for a job?' But that was the only thing I ever wanted to do."

KHAM

Beckham, age 19, stands with his Manchester United teammates before his UEFA Champions League debut, in a game against Galatasaray, December 7, 1994. Beckham would go on to score a goal in a 4–0 victory.

first things she noticed about him were how calm he was and how close he was to his family, even at the height of his stardom. Beckham was sometimes called a "mama's boy," but he felt no shame about it. The support he received from his family was what sustained him in his career.

Beckham is known for being loyal and conscientious in every task he takes on. He would spend hours on the field practicing the "bend," his famous long-range shot. However, his conscientiousness was not entirely apparent in his first summer job, gathering glasses at an open-air restaurant close to his home. The restaurant owner liked the calm young Beckham, but would repeatedly catch him engaged in heated conversations with both customers and coworkers. "What are you talking about?" the owner would ask. And Beckham would always reply, "Football!"

When he was eleven years old, Beckham won the Bobby Charlton Soccer Skills Competition for his exceptional ball-control ability. The winning prize was a training session with FC Barcelona, during which Beckham drew the attention of a Manchester United talent scout.

DAVID BECKHAM
DATE OF BIRTH: MAY 2, 1975
PLACE OF BIRTH: LONDON, ENGLAND
YOUTH CLUBS: RIDGEWAY ROVERS (1985–87), TOTTENHAM HOTSPUR (1987–91), BRIMSTOWN ROVERS (1989–91), MANCHESTER UNITED (1991–93)
SENIOR CLUBS: MANCHESTER UNITED (1992–2003), PRESTON NORTH END (1994–95), REAL MADRID (2003–07), LA GALAXY (2007–12), A.C. MILAN (2009), PARIS-SAINT GERMAIN (2013)
NATIONAL TEAM: ENGLAND (1996–2009)

Beckham got a step closer to fulfilling his dream of playing for Man U when he formally signed an agreement with the club's development league on his fourteenth birthday. He began playing as a trainee two years later. He helped the club win an FA Youth Cup against Crystal Palace his first season. Beckham's continued success as a trainee led to his first-team debut just months later, when he was subbed in during a League Cup match. Beckham signed on to the club as a professional in January 1993.

Though his professional career would see him traded to Real Madrid and LA Galaxy, and loaned to A.C. Milan, Beckham has never forgotten his Manchester United roots.

Objectively speaking, David Beckham perhaps never reached the highest summit of football. Three things, though, made Beckham into an international superstar, aside from his devastating right foot. First, he was the driving force of the invincible Manchester United team under the reign of manager Alex Ferguson. Second, he became a symbol of the globalization of soccer during his time as one of the famed Galacticos of Real Madrid, who helped bring soccer to an even higher level of popularity and influence. Third, his arrival on the LA Galaxy squad in 2007 helped establish Major League Soccer as a serious institution in the United States.

Abby Wambach is the only soccer star in this volume who learned to play the sport from a book. Her career—which includes two Olympic gold medals, one World Cup title, 184 international goals, and countless personal awards—began when her older sister Laura decided that she wanted to learn to play soccer. Their mother Judy had seven children altogether, and all of them were involved in one sport or another. None of them had any experience with soccer, though, so Judy visited the local library and brought home a book that explained the rules of the sport. The Wambach kids then began experimenting with this interesting new game—and for Abby Wambach it turned into a lifelong fascination.

Before the seven Wambach children began playing soccer, they were constantly up to something fun and exciting in their neighborhood of Pittsford, in Rochester, New York. And Abby, who was the youngest, would repeatedly get caught up in her siblings' adventures. She recalled that her brothers "would put me in goal when we played street hockey because I was the

ABBY WAM

At McDonald's, Abby cooked up creative ways to protect her fries from her hungry brothers. Matthew Wambach recalls one of her ingenious methods: "Her way of stopping us was to take a bite of every fry and set them down. Who wants to eat a half-bitten French fry?"

Wambach, age 24, celebrates after scoring the gold medal-winning goal in overtime for Team USA in the Summer Olympics in Athens, Greece, August 26, 2004.

BACH

Wambach, age 21, vies for possession of the ball in one of her first appearances in her professional career, March 30, 2002.

smallest, and I would have pucks flying at me." But it wasn't just street hockey—the siblings also loved lacrosse, basketball, and rollerblading. Their outdoor lifestyle was encouraged by their mother, who, Wambach says, would "lock us out of the house and tell us to go and play. We couldn't come in even if we needed to pee—we had to go in the bushes."

In this kind of competitive and energetic atmosphere Wambach would have excelled at any sport. She was tall and strong from an early age, which would work to her advantage on the field, yet it was her ambition that stood out the most.

"She was as competitive as you can get," Matthew, one of her brothers, said when asked to describe his successful sister during an interview in the New York Times. The first time he realized she was exceptionally gifted was during a game of catch football: "I threw the ball to one of the neighbors and Abby tackled him. She got up and he was on the ground, groaning. She was 11 or 12. I don't think he was ready to get blasted." After scoring twenty-seven goals in her first three rec-league games, she was immediately moved to a boys'

team that could better satisfy her competitive drive.

Abby herself told Yahoo! Sports how she came to acquire her special kind of grit: "My brothers and sisters always played with me on the same level and they never let me win until I was better than them and deserved it. Being in such a big family makes you humble. You might have a certain skill or talent but there is always someone who is better at something than you." Nevertheless, Wambach trained with such focus that eventually her talents outstripped the rest. Today Wambach may be one of the best soccer players in the world, but her family continues to be a motivating force in her life.

MARY ABIGAIL "ABBY" WAMBACH
DATE OF BIRTH: JUNE 2, 1980
PLACE OF BIRTH: ROCHESTER, NEW YORK
YOUTH CLUB: ROCHESTER SPIRIT (1995–97)
COLLEGE CLUB: UNIVERSITY OF FLORIDA (1998–2001)
SENIOR CLUBS: WASHINGTON FREEDOM (2002–03), WASHINGTON FREEDOM (2009–10), MAGICJACK (2011), WESTERN NEW YORK FLASH (2013–14)
NATIONAL TEAM: UNITED STATES (2001–15)

When Wambach was growing up, women's soccer was not as popular as it is today. Her first sports hero was basketball legend Michael Jordan, until she also found out about Michelle Akers, April Heinrichs, and Mia Hamm.

ZLATAN IBRAHIMOVIĆ

Zlatan sometimes like to provoke people with his boasting. But this is not simply arrogance or meaningless posturing—Zlatan is a humorist, and his boasts delight his fans. And besides, he's earned the right to brag, given his incredible journey from an impoverished Swedish neighborhood to the heights of international soccer.

Malmö is the third-largest city of Sweden, with a total population of 700,000, including the surrounding area. In the late 1960s, city officials began construction of a new neighborhood, Rosengård, which became home to many low-income families. These were joined later by immigrants and refugees, who were often poor themselves. In this hardscrabble neighborhood, the paths of two Balkan immigrants crossed, a Muslim

It soon became obvious that Zlatan had a great talent for soccer. However, for a long time he couldn't decide whether to focus on soccer or on the martial art of taekwondo. While his millions of fans must be glad that he ultimately chose soccer, there is no doubt that his martial arts skills contributed to his growth as a soccer player. For such a tall man (6 feet 7 inches), Zlatan is incredibly flexible, and some of his best goals look almost like ballet.

Zlatan, age 19, during an Ajax Amsterdam game against Sparta Rotterdam, October 1, 2001.

Zlatan, age 19, in uniform for Ajax Amsterdam, July 13, 2001.

boy from Bosnia named Sefik Ibrahimović and a Catholic girl from Croatia, Jurka Garvic, and they fell in love. They had three children together, among them Zlatan, born in 1981. Then Sefik and Jurka divorced, and Zlatan lived between their two homes. Life was hard, and sometimes the family needed assistance from social services to put food on the table. The couple eventually made peace with each other and had three more children together.

Zlatan's parents were strict, but he still had a considerable amount of freedom. He rode around the city on a bicycle with his friends, and they would find countless ways to entertain themselves. Zlatan had a strong personality and a rebellious nature that sometimes turned people against him. Schoolwork came easy to Zlatan, but he was never fully committed to his studies. If Zlatan was having trouble getting to or from practice, he would "borrow" a bicycle he found locked up on the street. He once even rode off on his coach's bike after practice, much to the coach's chagrin. He has implied that without his athletic gifts, especially in soccer, he might have ended up on the wrong side of the law.

ZLATAN IBRAHIMOVIĆ
DATE OF BIRTH: OCTOBER 3, 1981
PLACE OF BIRTH: MALMÖ, SWEDEN
YOUTH CLUBS: MALMÖ BI (1989–91), FBK BALKAN (1991–95), MALMÖ FF (1995–99)
SENIOR CLUBS: MALMÖ FF (1999–2001), AJAX (2001–04), JUVENTUS (2004–06), INTER MILAN (2006–09), BARCELONA (2009–10), A.C. MILAN (2010–12), PARIS-SAINT GERMAIN (2012–16), MANCHESTER UNITED (2016–18), LA GALAXY (2018)
NATIONAL TEAM: SWEDEN (2001–16)

On the soccer field in Rosengård, players were rewarded for their individual playing styles. Zlatan learned to emulate the effortless "ginga" moves of Brazilian stars like Romario and Ronaldo. Even decades later, Zlatan is known for his showmanship on the field. Zlatan is proud of his old neighborhood, and he often emphasizes that he is the "boy from Rosengård." In 2007, Zlatan helped fund repairs of an old soccer field in the area where he himself began practicing soccer at the age of four. There is an inscription on the entrance to the field that reads: "Here is my heart. Here is my history. Here is my game. Take it further. Zlatan."

As a teenager, Zlatan joined Malmö FF and attracted attention immediately. Arsenal manager Arsene Wenger heard about the promising soccer talent and invited Zlatan for a trial with the London superteam. Most seventeen-year-olds would have jumped at the opportunity to play with such an epic team, led by such a legendary manager, but this was not the case with young Zlatan. He later explained, "I turned him down. Zlatan doesn't do auditions."

CARLI LLOYD

Carli Lloyd's autobiography is aptly titled *When Nobody Was Watching*. While Lloyd's ambition as an athlete was never in question, she was somewhat overshadowed by bigger stars early in her career. She first managed to attract significant attention when she scored the winning goal at the 2008 Summer Olympics in Beijing. She repeated this feat at the 2012 Summer Olympics in London. Lloyd was already in her thirties when she had her greatest triumph yet, scoring a hat trick against Japan at the 2015 World Cup and clinching the American victory in the tournament. Finally she had shown the world what her combination of skill and passion could offer.

Lloyd was born in the working-class town of Delran, New Jersey, where family was all-important. She constantly involved herself in whatever sport was being played in the neighborhood, whether it was street hockey or basketball. She was mostly uninterested in traditional "girl" hobbies, and she quickly gave up on dance lessons. Lloyd received abundant support from her family as she grew up and took her first steps into the world of soccer. Her

Lloyd might seem like an unstoppable force, but fans may be surprised to learn that she nearly gave up soccer altogether at one point. Being cut from the U.S. women's national U-21 team was nearly too much for Lloyd to handle as a college player. It was hard to hear that she was not doing enough for her teammates on the field, and her defensive playing needed improvement.

But thankfully for her fans, Lloyd persevered. She began work with a new trainer, who helped to address her weaknesses. She credits the experience with teaching her to face criticism as a player and develop her character. Like all the best players, she used a moment of adversity as motivation to improve.

Lloyd, age 24, in a friendly match against Chinese Taipei, October 1, 2006.

Lloyd, age 25, in her first World Cup game against North Korea, September 11, 2007.

mother recalls that Lloyd enjoyed playing soccer with boys and "showed a lot of ability from an early age, but she also has always worked hard." Lloyd remembers that she "used to kick the ball up against the curb for hours upon hours." Then she would collect every soccer ball in sight and head to the field to work on her shooting technique.

But Lloyd also wishes she had been pushed harder in her youth so she could have reached her goals sooner: "I thought of myself as this princess who could do no wrong and that wasn't the case. I never looked in the mirror and said to myself: I need to be better." (Nevertheless, Lloyd was twice named the Girls' High School Player of the Year by the *Philadelphia Inquirer*.)

Now she pushes herself as hard as she can. In her autobiography, she writes,

"I always train on Christmas Day. . . . It's an affirmation of how committed I am, how I am ready to go even on the most special holiday of the year."

In the international soccer scene, the number 10 jersey carries a special meaning. This was the number that belonged to the legendary Pelé, who combined the best aspects of playmaker and attacker, both setting up goals for teammates and scoring goals himself. Later, Maradona would also sport the number 10 jersey. It is now usually awarded to the most important forward on a team. So when Carli Lloyd chose the number 10 for herself, was it an indication of how she and others rated her performance on the field?

Not exactly. She chose the number because it belonged to the baseball player Darren Daulton. Originally she had wanted number 4, which was baseballer Lenny Dykstra's number, but it was taken. Lloyd then said to herself: "Alright, well, I like Darren Daulton, so I'm going to go with 10." After that the number simply stuck with her.

Christine Sinclair hated soccer and found the idea of chasing a soccer ball around a field totally boring. She just wanted to sit by the field and look at its beautiful green grass. But then the coach ordered her to get up and make herself useful to the team. So Sinclair sprang to her feet and dashed toward her teammates. After all, a four-year-old obeys her coach—especially if the coach also happens to be her mother!

CHRISTINE SINCLAIR

Growing up, Sinclair and her older brother Mike had a love-hate relationship. They would sometimes have to be sent to their separate rooms for fighting. Yet when their parents came to check on them, they would find the two siblings in the same room. One of them had snuck out of his or her window and into the other's, so they could both be grounded together.

Sinclair, age 20, dribbles past the Swedish
defense during the FIFA Women's World Cup
semifinals, October 5, 2003.

Sinclair, age 18, as a
freshman player for the
University of Portland Pilots,
November 18, 2001.

Many of Latin America's greatest soccer legends grew up in the poorest conditions. For these players, soccer was one of the only available paths out of poverty. In North America, however, soccer is mainly a middle-class sport. But the struggle to rise to the top of the game can be just as fierce.

Christine Sinclair, for example, was born to a middle-class family in Burnaby, a city just outside Vancouver, where everybody played soccer. Two of her uncles on her father's side were members of the Canadian national team. And, as we have seen, her mother was her first coach. Over time, Sinclair began to appreciate the sport that she had initially refused to play, and in fact become so quick and skilled on the field that she was playing with kids two and three years older, mostly boys. "It was a constant struggle to show that I belonged with them," she later said. In fact, she excelled at baseball as well, but at the age of eleven she finally decided to focus all her energy on soccer. Just five years later, she joined the ranks of the Canadian women's national team. At barely sixteen years old, she was already racking up an impressive number of goals.

CHRISTINE MARGARET SINCLAIR
DATE OF BIRTH: JUNE 12, 1983
PLACE OF BIRTH: BURNABY, BRITISH COLUMBIA, CANADA
YOUTH CLUB: BURNABY GIRLS SOCCER CLUB (1994–2000)
COLLEGE CLUB: UNIVERSITY OF PORTLAND PILOTS (2001–05)
SENIOR CLUBS: FC GOLD PRIDE (2009–10), WESTERN NEW YORK FLASH (2011–12), PORTLAND THORNS FC (2013–)
NATIONAL TEAM: CANADA (2000–)

Christine Sinclair was eighteen when she realized what a powerful athlete she was. She was in Portugal with the Canadian national team, playing in the Algarve Cup tournament, and their coach Even Pellerud was delivering a pep talk in the hotel lobby before a game. At one point, he said, "The best player in the world is on our team." Sinclair was surprised, and looked at the other faces in the lobby. "Which of my teammates could he think so highly of?" she thought—and then she figured out that he was talking about her.

Whether Sinclair is in fact the world's greatest female soccer player remains debatable. A few other names come to mind, but when Sinclair was in her best form, she definitely ranked among the top five—which is quite an achievement for someone who could hardly be bothered with the sport in the first place.

MARTA
VIEIRA DA SILVA

In Brazil, everybody loves soccer, and the very best players are idolized almost as gods—at least if they happen to be male. Recognition was harder to come by for Marta Vieira da Silva, who was born in 1986 in the Brazilian town of Dois Riachos. Women's soccer was then still in its infancy in Brazil, and Marta was viewed with suspicion for her devotion to a sport that, in her hometown at least, was exclusively played by boys.

Marta grew up in a poor household and was raised by a single mother who had to work long hours in order to make ends meet. As a result, Marta spent much of her time at her grandmother's place, where many of her cousins, mostly boys, would also stay. Marta remembers that they and the neighborhood kids "would pick up a couple of large stones and set up a sort of improvised goal. And that's how my interest in football started growing."

Marta loved soccer from the very first moment she was passed the ball. She was both swift and dexterous and immediately exhibited great talent for the sport. But would these talents be allowed to blossom? Marta has spoken about the disapproval she had to endure even from the people closest to her: "Obviously, most of my family members didn't approve of me playing." According to traditional Brazilian ideas about gender roles, a girl playing soccer was not "natural." Nevertheless, Marta fearlessly kept

Marta, age 17, celebrates during the opening round of the FIFA Women's World Cup 2003, the first of Marta's career, September 21, 2003.

MARTA VIEIRA DA SILVA

DATE OF BIRTH: FEBRUARY 19, 1986

PLACE OF BIRTH: DOIS RIACHOS, ALAGOAS, BRAZIL

YOUTH CLUB: CSA (1999)

SENIOR CLUBS: VASCO DA GAMA (2000–02), SANTA CRUZ (2002–04), UMEÅ IK (2004–08), LOS ANGELES SOL (2009), SANTOS (2009–10), FC GOLD PRIDE (2010), SANTOS (2011), WESTERN NEW YORK FLASH (2011), TYRESÖ FF (2012–14), FC ROSENGÅRD (2014–17), ORLANDO PRIDE (2017–)

NATIONAL TEAM: BRAZIL (2002–)

Marta, age 17, slips past the Norwegian defender during Brazil's Group B match in the FIFA Women's World Cup, September 24, 2003.

playing. Often she was the only girl among dozens of boys. She was even banned from one youth tournament when the coach of another team complained about the presence of a female player.

Thankfully, coach Helena Pacheco, one of the leaders in developing women's soccer in Brazil, got wind of Marta's talents and invited her to join the women's team of Vasco da Gama in Rio de Janeiro. Then, when Marta was just eighteen, she signed with a powerful Swedish club for whom she scored a whopping 210 goals in 103 games! The rest is history. At twenty, she was named FIFA Women's World Player of the Year, a title she has now won six times, more than anyone ever before, male or female.

When Marta was just fourteen, she was offered the opportunity to travel to Rio de Janeiro to join the Vasco da Gama women's team. However, when she had arrived at the bus station and was about to embark on the long journey from Dois Riachos to Rio, she was suddenly struck with an overwhelming sense of doubt. Should she abandon her family to chase a dream that even close relatives deemed hopeless? "A girl playing professional soccer? Such nonsense!"

Years later, Marta wrote a letter to her fourteen-year-old self and read it aloud on a television series on women's soccer. She wrote, "Dear fourteen-year-old Marta, I know what you're thinking. I know what you're feeling. You got weird looks and mean comments every day, just because you were a girl, a girl who loved football." But, she continued, "This bus is going to take you to your dream. . . . Get on that bus!"

LIONEL MESSI

Many of the world's greatest soccer players had difficult childhoods. The Brazilian genius Rivaldo's family was so poor that he lost some of his teeth due to malnutrition. Another Brazilian legend, Garrincha ("little bird"), was born with a deformed spine, but he went on to become the key player on the team that won the 1962 World Cup. Yet no other soccer great has a story to equal that of Lionel "Leo" Messi.

Messi was born in the city of Rosario in Argentina in 1987. His family wasn't quite struggling, but they weren't rich, either—they had just enough to make ends meet. Messi was always a short kid, but everyone expected him to undergo a growth spurt at some point and reach

Though Messi's family was not affluent, they possessed something much more valuable, namely, a close, supportive bond. This kept Messi from getting into trouble, as many young men in his neighborhood did. For instance, another local boy his age, named Gustavo Rodas, was nearly as talented, and everyone saw a bright future for him. But Rodas's family was unable to offer him the same kind of support Messi received from his, and after a promising start, he has nearly disappeared from soccer history.

Messi, age 19, cuts through a line of Getafe defenders to score in a Copa del Ray semifinal between FC Barcelona and Getafe, April 18, 2007.

Messi, age 17, leaps for possession of the ball against Egypt's Abellah Gala during the FIFA World Youth Championship Match, June 17, 2005.

a normal height. He began playing soccer when he was four, and quickly exhibited great promise.

When he was ten years old, however, Messi was still only as big as an average five- or six-year-old. He was taken to a specialist, who diagnosed him with a growth hormone deficiency. The doctors estimated that he would probably not grow taller than 4 feet 9 inches. At that height, it would be impossible for him to play soccer at a pro-fessional level.

The treatment for Messi's condition required daily injections, which the young boy learned to give himself. However, the cost of the treatment was too high for his family to afford on their own. The soccer team River Plate in Buenos Aires offered to pay for the treatment if the outstanding youngster would agree to join their youth squad. But then Argentina was suddenly hit by an economic collapse, and River Plate was forced to make cuts to their budget, including the payments for Messi's treat-ment. Once again it seemed that Messi

LIONEL ANDRÉS MESSI
DATE OF BIRTH: JUNE 24, 1987
PLACE OF BIRTH: ROSARIO, ARGENTINA
YOUTH CLUBS: NEWELL'S OLD BOYS
   (1994–2000), BARCELONA (2001–04)
SENIOR CLUB: BARCELONA (2004–)
NATIONAL TEAM: ARGENTINA (2005–)

would never be able to reach the heights he dreamed of.

Thankfully, the story was far from over. Messi's family had relatives in Catalonia, and they brought the young player to the attention of the powerhouse team Bar-celona. Messi and his father traveled to Barcelona, and manager Carles Rexach only needed to watch the boy play for a couple of minutes to realize that the team simply had to get him on board. So Messi moved to Barcelona, and the team funded his treatment. He would never be a giant, but he did eventually reach the height of 5 feet 7 inches—enough to blossom into the greatest soccer player of modern times, and maybe of all time.

For many soccer geniuses, it is their father who first interests them in the sport and supports their development. But in Messi's case, it was his grandmother Celia who got him into soccer and encouraged him along. She often took care of him while his parents were at work and his older siblings were at school. Messi was a calm boy who rarely got excited. One day, however, a soccer ball crossed Messi's path, and he immediately became possessed by it. His grandmother then took him to a local youth team and asked if Messi could play. The coach said Messi was too small and too young, but his grandmother promised to take him off the field if he started crying. Messi then entered the field and dribbled past one taller boy after the other. The coach and the grandmother looked at each other in surprise—and a legend was born.

ALEX MORGAN

Alex Morgan is one of the few superstars in this book who was fortunate enough to grow up in a close-knit family that had the means to support her soccer journey from the very start. That doesn't mean she put any less effort into her ascent to the top of American soccer. On the contrary, Morgan has always been defined by her determination, focus, and diligence.

Morgan grew up in Diamond Bar, a suburb of Los Angeles, and was the youngest of three daughters. She played a multitude of sports with her sisters, and they would dash enthusiastically through the neighborhood, from one yard to the next.

Morgan turned out to be strong and quick on her feet, and she possessed a type of cunning and agility suited for a wide range of

Morgan isn't just a fierce player on the field—she's also a fierce champion for gender equality. After the U.S. Women's World Cup win in 2015, she and four other players turned their attention to #EqualPlayEqualPay, a campaign highlighting the fact that players on the U.S. women's national team were paid only one-quarter what players on the men's team were, despite earning more for the U.S. Soccer Federation. Morgan explained the fight was "for all the little girls around the world who deserve the same respect as well as the boys. They deserve a voice, and if we as professional athletes don't leverage the voices we have, we are letting them down. We will not let them down."

Morgan, age 21, celebrates a goal for the
California Golden Bears of UC Berkeley,
October 17, 2010.

Morgan, age 19, makes a run for the goal in the Women's U-20 World Cup final, December 7, 2008. The US would go on to win 2–1.

sports. For a time her coaches encouraged her to focus on sprinting, because they thought she might become a track star. She excelled in volleyball, basketball, and softball, too. But at the age of fourteen, she made the decision to focus entirely on soccer, a sport that draws on all her best qualities: speed, agility, strength, and cunning.

Morgan says that owes her success to her parents. Pamela Morgan worked a full-time job and studied for an MBA while Alex was growing up, but she always made time for her daughter's soccer games. She attended every match, loudly cheered for her daughter's team, and brought halftime snacks for the girls.

Morgan's father, Michael, was clueless about soccer when his daughter first got into the sport, but when her interest became serious, he immersed himself in soccer and later served as both a referee and a coach. He also worked full-time, as a construction engineer, but he always showed up to take his daughter to practice on time.

When Morgan was seventeen, and had just been invited to the Olympic Development Program in Southern California,

ALEXANDRA PATRICIA MORGAN
DATE OF BIRTH: JULY 2, 1989
PLACE OF BIRTH: SAN DIMAS, CALIFORNIA
YOUTH CLUB: CYPRESS ELITE (2003–07)
COLLEGE CLUB: CALIFORNIA GOLDEN BEARS (2007–10)
SENIOR CLUBS: WESTERN NEW YORK FLASH (2011), SEATTLE SOUNDERS WOMEN (2012), PORTLAND THORNS FC (2013–15), ORLANDO PRIDE (2016–), LYON (2017)
NATIONAL TEAM: UNITED STATES (2010–)

she suffered a serious injury to her right knee that threatened her career. Morgan's parents reacted immediately and did everything in their power to convince one of the world's best orthopedic surgeons to operate on her knee. And they stuck by her every day during her intense five-month rehabilitation program.

Speaking of her family's support, Morgan has said, "When you score your biggest goals and turn around, you'll always see family members . . . jumping up and down, going nuts, showing you love. That's special. Don't ever take that for granted."

Along with her achievements on the field, Morgan has been an outspoken advocate for the sport of soccer. She has written a series of novels for young readers called The Kicks, which focuses on soccer, friendship, and growing up. The Kicks has also been turned into a streaming TV show.

Neymar was born in 1992 in the Brazilian mountain village of Mogi das Cruzes. His father, Neymar da Silva Santos Sr., played soccer for a number of professional teams, although he never became a star.

When Neymar was four months old, his family was driving along a dangerous mountain road on a stormy day. They were on the way to visit his mother Nadine's parents, who lived in the beach town of Sao Vincente. The hard rain caused poor visibility on the road, and suddenly another car appeared out of nowhere, heading toward them in the

NEYMAR
DA SILVA SANTOS JR.

Growing up, Neymar was often called "Juninho" ("Junior") by his family members, because he had the same name as his father. But when he joined a senior team, he decided to call himself Neymar Junior, rather than simply Juninho. This was probably a wise decision, because it kept him from being confused with other Brazilian soccer stars like Juninho Paulista, a member of the 2002 World Cup team, or the free-kick specialist Juninho Pernambucano, who was part of the 2006 World Cup team.

Neymar, age 18, celebrates after his goal in a friendly match between Brazil and the U.S., August 10, 2010.

55

Neymar, age 19, during the FIFA
Club World Cup semifinal match
between Santos and Kashiwa
Reysol, December 14, 2011.

wrong lane. Neymar Sr. tried to swerve out of the way, but it was too late, and the cars crashed into each other.

After the accident, Neymar Sr. was stuck under the steering wheel with badly injured legs. Somehow he managed to wriggle free, and he and his wife crawled out the rear of their badly damaged car. But Neymar Jr. was nowhere to be seen. His parents shouted his name and desperately searched the area, fearing the worst.

In the end, Neymar Jr. was found in his little car seat with a tiny scratch on his forehead, still smiling. It was a close call, and that day soccer fans around the world almost lost a future hero.

His family later moved to Sao Vicente. One day Neymar Sr. was playing soccer on the beach there with his team at the time. Nadine sat watching the game with the six-year-old Neymar Jr. on her lap. Eventually Neymar Jr. got bored and began playing with a stray soccer ball.

By chance, Betinho, a talent scout for the great team Santos, was also there to watch the game. (Betinho had previously discovered one of the most popular players of that time, Robinho.) Watching Neymar Jr. play

around with the ball, Betinho was struck by his precocious talent and coordination. He wondered, though, whether the boy could ever develop the power necessary to join the ranks of the world's greatest. But then Neymar Jr. "started doing tricks with the ball, tricks that no average kid could make," Betinho said. "I was in shock."

Neymar joined the Santos FC youth system at age eleven. His star rose quickly as a junior player, and Real Madrid tried to recruit him when he was fourteen. Yet Santos managed to hang on to the sought-after player, and he made his senior debut for the team in 2009. His story was just beginning.

Betinho took Neymar to play futsal, or indoor soccer. This fast-paced game offered Neymar the perfect opportunity to develop his agility, speed, and cunning. Neymar attracted attention from a young age for his incredible ability to dash from one end of the field to the other, and his phenomenal dribbling skills, which allowed to him to break through defensive walls and take a shot while the goalkeeper was still trying to figure out where it would come from.

The decade from 2008 to 2018 was the era of Messi and Cristiano Ronaldo. Even Neymar has yet to reach their level. But now it seems that that their rightful heir has been discovered.

Kylian Mbappé, born in Paris in 1998, has truly international roots. His mother, Fayza Lamari, was born in Algeria and later moved to France, where she became a handball star. His father, Wilfried Mbappé, was born in Cameroon and also has Nigerian ancestry. Wilfried was a soccer player and later a coach for a small team on

KYLIAN MBAPPÉ

Many great players have special ways to celebrate goals. Messi, for example, raises his fingers to the sky and looks toward the heavens, in tribute to his deceased grandmother. Mbappé has another way of celebrating. He poses with his arms crossed and his thumbs up. This is a good-natured tribute to his younger brother Ethan. "He celebrated like that every time he beat the hell out of me on PlayStation FIFA games," Kylian says.

Mbappé, age 17, playing for AS Monaco during a French Ligue 1 match against Paris Saint-Germain, March 20, 2016.

Mbappé celebrates France's World Cup win against Croatia, July 15, 2018. It was during the tournament that the 19-year-old Mbappé became the youngest French goalscorer in World Cup history.

KYLIAN MBAPPÉ LOTTIN
DATE OF BIRTH: DECEMBER 20, 1998
PLACE OF BIRTH: PARIS, FRANCE
YOUTH CLUBS: AS BONDY (2004–13), MONACO (2013–15)
SENIOR CLUBS: MONACO (2015–17), PARIS-SAINT GERMAIN (2017–)
NATIONAL TEAM: FRANCE (2017–)

the outskirts of Paris, AS Bondy. Mbappé's adopted brother, Jirès Kembo Ekeko, is from the Congo. Kembo is ten year older, so he was always Kylian's role model growing up. Kembo Ekoko now plays for the strong Turkish team Bursaspor.

Mbappé's family and his first coaches were quick to realize that he was gifted not only with incredible soccer talents but also with the focus and ambition necessary to develop his skills. "You could say that Kylian was born here at this club," Atmane Air-ouche, president of AS Bondy, has said. In a way, Mbappé had been with the team since he was a young child, tagging along with his father and learning about every aspect of the sport: "When we played games, just before kick-off you'd see a two-year-old walk in with a ball and he'd sit with us to listen to the team talks."

In an interview with the BBC, Antonio Riccardi, under-13 coach at Bondy, also spoke fondly of the young Mbappé's obvious talent and familiarity with the game: "The first time I coached him was when he was six years old. Just a few months after he had started playing here . . . you could tell he was different. Kylian could do much more than the other children. His dribbling was already fantastic and he was much faster than the others."

The boy was obviously special, and his positive attitude is a big factor in his success. He knows how to enjoy life as much as he enjoys soccer. When he was playing a youth game, he once said to one of his teammates, "I'll take the ball in two minutes and I'll score!" And exactly one hundred and twenty seconds later, he recovered the ball and dribbled past four or five players, finally scoring a goal with a superb flick. His teammate just laughed: "It meant that he had the ability to do it since the beginning of the match. Kylian makes things look easy."

Like any handball star, Mbappé's mother is tough as nails, and she is very protective of her son. When she learned that his Brazilian teammates at Paris-Saint Germain, Neymar and Dani Alves, had begun to tease him, she was furious. (They had nicknamed him Donatello, after the Teenage Mutant Ninja Turtles character.) Fayza is a staunch believer in discipline and team solidarity in sports, and she demanded that PSG reprimand the Brazilians. PSG responded that the teasing was lighthearted in nature—but following Mbappé's performance at the 2018 World Cup, there's little chance anyone will dare pull his leg again.